LOOK!

LOOK!

by Ted Lewin

I Like to Read®

Holiday House / New York

For Gaby, who loves books

I LIKE TO READ is a registered trademark of Holiday House, Inc.

Copyright © 2013 by Ted Lewin
All Rights Reserved
HOLIDAY HOUSE is registered in the U.S. Patent and Trademark Office.
Printed and Bound in November 2013 at Tien Wah Press, Johor Bahru, Johor, Malaysia.
The artwork was created with pencil and watercolor
on Strathmore bristol.
www.holidayhouse.com
3 5 7 9 10 8 6 4 2

Library of Congress Cataloging-in-Publication Data
Lewin, Ted.
Look! / Ted Lewin. — 1st ed.
p. cm. — (An I like to read)
Summary: "An elephant eats, giraffes drink, a warthog digs, and
a boy plays, reads, and dreams."— Provided by publisher.
ISBN 978-0-8234-2607-2 (hardcover)
1. Animals—Africa—Juvenile literature. 2. Animal ecology—Africa—Juvenile literature. I. Title.
QL49.L3875 2013
590.22'2—dc23
2011049607

ISBN 978-0-8234-3059-8 (paperback)
GRL D

Look!

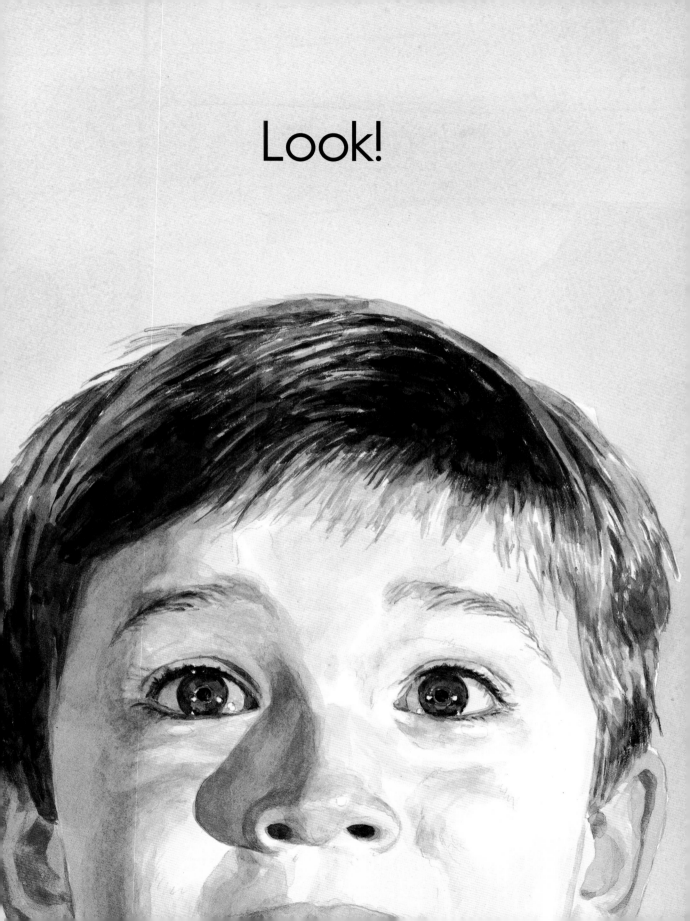

Look! An elephant eats.

Look! Giraffes drink.

Look! A warthog digs.

Look! A gorilla hides.

Look! Wild dogs listen.

Look!

Zebras run.

Look! Monkeys sit.

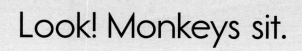

Look! Hippos splash.

Look! A rhino naps.

Look! A boy plays.

A boy reads.

A boy dreams.

I Like to Read® Books
You will like all of them!

Paperback and Hardcover

Boy, Bird, and Dog by David McPhail

Dinosaurs Don't, Dinosaurs Do by Steve Björkman

The Lion and the Mice
by Rebecca Emberley and Ed Emberley

See Me Run by Paul Meisel
A Theodor Seuss Geisel Award Honor Book

Hardcover

Car Goes Far by Michael Garland

Fish Had a Wish by Michael Garland

The Fly Flew In by David Catrow

I Have a Garden by Bob Barner

I Will Try by Marilyn Janovitz

Late Nate in a Race by Emily Arnold McCully

Look! by Ted Lewin

Mice on Ice
by Rebecca Emberley and Ed Emberley

Pig Has a Plan by Ethan Long

Sam and the Big Kids by Emily Arnold McCully

See Me Dig by Paul Meisel

Sick Day by David McPhail

You Can Do It! by Betsy Lewin

Visit holidayhouse.com to read more
about I Like to Read® Books.

I Like to Read® Books in Paperback
You will like all of them!

Visit http://www.holidayhouse.com/I-Like-to-Read/
for more about I Like to Read® books, including
flash cards, reproducibles, and the complete list of titles.